EXPLORING COUNTRIES

Laos

by Emily Rose Oachs

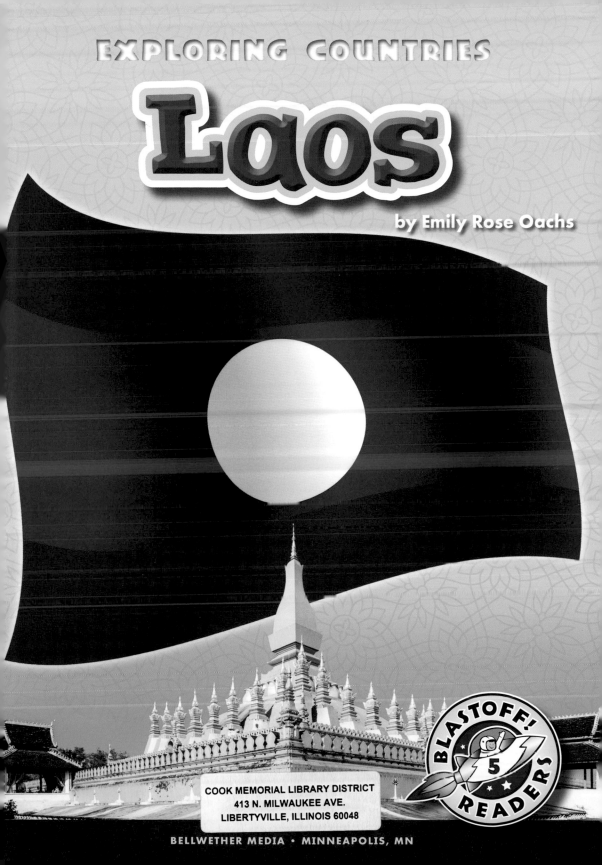

BLASTOFF! 5 READERS

BELLWETHER MEDIA · MINNEAPOLIS, MN

Note to Librarians, Teachers, and Parents:

Blastoff! Readers are carefully developed by literacy experts and combine standards-based content with developmentally appropriate text.

Level 1 provides the most support through repetition of high-frequency words, light text, predictable sentence patterns, and strong visual support.

Level 2 offers early readers a bit more challenge through varied simple sentences, increased text load, and less repetition of high-frequency words.

Level 3 advances early-fluent readers toward fluency through increased text and concept load, less reliance on visuals, longer sentences, and more literary language.

Level 4 builds reading stamina by providing more text per page, increased use of punctuation, greater variation in sentence patterns, and increasingly challenging vocabulary.

Level 5 encourages children to move from "learning to read" to "reading to learn" by providing even more text, varied writing styles, and less familiar topics.

Whichever book is right for your reader, Blastoff! Readers are the perfect books to build confidence and encourage a love of reading that will last a lifetime!

This edition first published in 2017 by Bellwether Media, Inc.

No part of this publication may be reproduced in whole or in part without written permission of the publisher. For information regarding permission, write to Bellwether Media, Inc., Attention: Permissions Department, 5357 Penn Avenue South, Minneapolis, MN 55419.

Library of Congress Cataloging-in-Publication Data

Names: Oachs, Emily Rose, author.
Title: Laos / by Emily Rose Oachs.
Description: Minneapolis, MN : Bellwether Media, Inc., 2017. | Series: Blastoff! Readers. Exploring Countries | Includes bibliographical references and index. | Audience: Grades 3-7.
Identifiers: LCCN 2015049959 | ISBN 9781626174047 (hardcover : alk. paper)
Subjects: LCSH: Laos–Juvenile literature.
Classification: LCC DS555.3 .O23 2017 | DDC 959.4–dc23
LC record available at http://lccn.loc.gov/2015049959

Printed in the United States of America, North Mankato, MN.

Contents

Laos rests in the center of Southeast Asia. It spreads over 91,429 square miles (236,800 square kilometers). Because it is **landlocked**, Laos only touches other countries. China lies to the north. Vietnam is Laos's eastern neighbor, and Cambodia borders southern Laos. The Mekong River forms most of Laos's western boundary. It separates Laos from Thailand and Burma (Myanmar).

Vientiane is Laos's capital and largest city. It sits on the banks of the Mekong River. Pakxe, Savannakhet, and Luang Prabang are other major Laotian cities. They also stand along the Mekong River.

China

Vietnam

Burma
(Myanmar)

Laos

Vientiane

Mekong
River

Thailand

Cambodia

N
W   E
S

Did you know?
The Mekong River is Southeast Asia's
longest river. It winds for 2,700 miles
(4,345 kilometers)!

Rugged mountains define Laos's landscape. The Annamite Range crosses central Laos and its eastern border. Woodlands cover nearly half of the country. **Tropical rain forests** blanket northern mountains. In the south are forests of bamboo and banana trees. Three high **plateaus** offer grassy farmland. **Lowlands** surround the Mekong River. Some years the river floods these areas.

Laos has hot temperatures year round. The mountains are cooler than lowlands. From May to October is Laos's rainy season. During that time, **monsoons** blow heavy rain into the country. The dry season lasts from November to April.

A vast system of caves hides beneath the earth's surface in central Laos. The caves were formed by rain seeping into cracks in limestone. Over time, this water carved small passages into the stone. Eventually, the water widened these passages into massive caves.

Among the longest and most famous caves is the Tham Kong Lo. A river winds through this spectacular 4-mile (7-kilometer) long cavern. It flows past many beautiful rock formations. The Pak Ou Caves are carved into cliffs overlooking the Mekong River. For hundreds of years, Laotians have stored thousands of important Buddha statues there.

Did you know?

In the 1960s and 1970s, thousands of Laotians lived in the northeastern Viengxay Caves. They were seeking protection from bombings.

douc langur

Many of Laos's wild forests offer safe places for **endangered** animals to find shelter. Douc langurs and leaf monkeys swing through the treetops. Small, rare sun bears hide in wooded lowlands. Asian elephants lumber through the rain forests. In mountain forests roam herds of large wild cattle, called gaur. Tigers and clouded leopards prowl the same forests for prey.

sun bear

Asian elephant

tokay gecko

! fun fact

Tree-dwelling tokay geckos can reach 14 inches (35 centimeters) in length. Some Laotians own them as pets to keep their homes insect-free!

Deer-like saolas are only found in the Annamite Mountains. The lowlands and rain forests are home to Burmese pythons and king cobras. Buzzards and black-headed woodpeckers also dwell in the rain forests. Kingfishers and hornbills nest throughout the country.

Did you know?

More than 80 languages are spoken in Laos! Lao is the country's official language, but many Laotians speak other local languages.

fun fact

To greet one another, Laotians place their hands palm to palm in front of their chest. This is called the *nop*.

Nearly 7 million people call Laos home. Many **ethnic** groups live in the country. Each has its own language and **traditions**. These ethnic groups are divided into three main groups.

The Lowland Lao make up two out of every three people. They live on **plains** and in river valleys, often in small villages or cities. Most practice Buddhism. The other two groups are the Midslope and Highland Lao. They make their homes in mountain villages. These peoples often practice **animist** religions.

Speak Lao!

Laotians use Lao script when they write. However, Lao words can be written in English to help you read them aloud.

English	Lao	How to say it
hello	sabaidi	sa-BY-dee
goodbye	laa gawn	LAH goan
yes	jao	jow
no	baw	baw
please	khaluna	kah-LOO-na
thank you	khawp jai	cop jai
friend	muu	moo

Most Laotians live in scattered villages in the mountains and plains. **Rural** families farm the land surrounding villages to survive. Traditional Lao houses stand high off the ground, on stilts. This keeps them safe from flooding. During the rainy season, muddy roads make it difficult to reach villages by car.

Less than half of Laotians live in the country's few large cities. They live in small houses made of bricks and concrete. Recently, more Laotians have begun to move near the Mekong River. There, larger towns offer more jobs, better health care, and better education.

Where People Live in Laos

cities
38.6%

countryside
61.4%

At age 6, most Laotians enter primary school. Students learn to read and write in the Lao language. They also take classes in math, social studies, art, and physical education. In rural areas, sometimes students do not enter school until they are 10 years old. Schools also do not always have enough teachers. Students from many different grades may be taught in the same classroom.

After five years, many students move on to seven years of secondary school. There, students receive training for a specific job or continue their general studies. Then students find jobs or enroll in university.

Working

Where People Work in Laos

services
43.5%

industry
33.4%

agriculture
23.1%

Did you know?

In the lowlands, farmers plant rice in flooded fields called paddies. Mountain farmers cut down large areas of forest each year. Then they plant rice and other crops in these fresh fields.

Farming is very important in Laos. Most Laotians own or work on farms. Rice is the country's main crop. Farmers also grow corn, coffee beans, sugarcane, and vegetables. They raise cattle, pigs, and water buffalo. Many Laotians rely on their farms to produce food for their families. Mountain families also gather items from the forests, such as fruits, honey, and mushrooms.

Laos's lands are filled with many **natural resources**. Teak, bamboo, and rattan are harvested from its thick forests. Workers mine for copper, gold, and tin. Then, they **export** them to other countries. Many Laotians have **service jobs**. They work in hospitals, banks, restaurants, schools, and shops.

kataw

Both children and adults enjoy playing the sport *kataw*. Players bat a rattan ball back and forth over a net. They can only hit the ball with their heads or feet. Children often play the sport in schoolyards. *Muay Lao* is a **martial art** similar to kickboxing. Laotians enjoy matches broadcast on television. Kids also love to watch and play soccer.

Rural Laotians play folk music using the *khaen*, a traditional mouth organ. As the music plays, people dance a popular folk dance called *lam wong*. Laotian pop and hip-hop are recent musical styles. They are popular with young people.

khaen players

Did you know?

In Laos, people usually eat their meals while sitting on the floor.

Sticky rice is a **staple** in Laotian diets. Laotians eat it with their fingers from a small basket. Sometimes they use the rice to dip into or scoop up other food. Other times they buy it from street carts to eat plain as a snack.

Larb is a favorite Laotian dish. It is a spicy meat salad made with chicken, fresh herbs, and fish sauce. Laotians serve it with sticky rice and raw vegetables or lettuce. *Khao piak sen*, a noodle soup, is a common breakfast. Raw, shredded green papaya, tomatoes, garlic, chilies, fish sauce, and lime make up Laos's *tam mak houng*.

larb

sticky rice

fun fact
More sticky rice is eaten in Laos than anywhere else in the world. Each person eats an average of 345 pounds (156 kilograms) every year!

Each April, the Lao New Year, *Pi Mai Lao*, is an important holiday. To prepare, homes, temples, and Buddha statues are cleaned. Laotians then celebrate with parades, bright banners, and performances of traditional music and dance. People also empty small water buckets on others. They believe rinsing people with water gives them a fresh start to the new year.

On December 2, Laos holds its National Day celebrations. These honor the date the country replaced its king with **communist** leaders in 1975. Each May, Laos holds its Rocket Festival. To celebrate, people launch homemade bamboo rockets into the sky to summon rain!

fun fact

On some important events and holidays, such as weddings and the new year, Laotians hold *baci* celebrations. They tie white cotton strings around their wrists. These bring good luck!

Pi Mai Lao

Buddhism

Did you know?

In the lowlands, a Buddhist temple, called a wat, stands at the center of most villages. People gather there for prayer, festivals, and village meetings.

About two out of every three Laotians practice Buddhism. They give thanks to the Buddha, follow his teachings, and **meditate** to reflect on themselves and the world. For most Laotians, Buddhism is at the center of their lives.

Some Laotians make daily offerings to **monks**. At sunrise, they kneel on the ground as monks pass by. They drop rice or fruit into the bowls the monks carry. Laotians do this to show respect to the monks, and the monks rely on these donations to eat each day. Laotians' commitment to Buddhism has helped shape their country's culture and traditions.

Fast Facts About Laos

Laos's Flag

The Laotian flag has three horizontal stripes with red on the top and bottom and blue in the middle. In the center is a white circle. The red stands for the blood Laotians lost while fighting for independence. Blue stands for wealth, well-being, and the Mekong River. The white circle represents the moon's reflection. It also symbolizes the country's unity and the hope for a successful future. The flag was adopted in 1975.

Official Name: Lao People's Democratic Republic

Area: 91,429 square miles (236,800 square kilometers); Laos is the 84th largest country in the world.

Capital City:	Vientiane
Other Important Cities:	Pakxe, Savannakhet, Luang Prabang
Population:	6,911,544 (July 2015)
Official Language:	Lao
National Holiday:	National Day (December 2)
Religions:	Buddhism (66.8%), Christianity (1.5%), Other (31.7%)
Major Industries:	agriculture, mining, electric power, tourism
Natural Resources:	gemstones, gold, gypsum, timber, tin, hydropower
Manufactured Products:	food products, clothing, bricks, nails
Farm Products:	rice, sweet potatoes, peanuts, cotton, tea, coffee beans, water buffalo, pigs
Unit of Money:	kip; the kip is divided into 100 att.

Glossary

animist—based in nature and the belief that spirits exist in the natural environment

communist—following a form of government where the government controls all land and business in a country

endangered—at risk of becoming extinct

ethnic—related to a group of people with a specific cultural background

export—to sell to a different country

landlocked—completely surrounded by land

lowlands—areas of land that are lower than the surrounding land

martial art—a style and technique of fighting and self-defense

meditate—to quietly think or reflect for religious purposes or relaxation

monks—men who have given up all their belongings to become part of a specific religious community

monsoons—winds that shift direction each season; monsoons bring heavy rain.

natural resources—materials in the earth that are taken out and used to make products or fuel

plains—large areas of flat land

plateaus—areas of flat, raised land

rural—related to the countryside

service jobs—jobs that perform tasks for people or businesses

staple—a widely used food or other item

traditions—customs, ideas, or beliefs handed down from one generation to the next

tropical rain forests—thick, green forests that lie in the hot and wet areas near the equator